THE BUDDHA WONDERS
IF SHE IS HAVING A MID-LIFE CRISIS

THE BUDDHA WONDERS
IF SHE IS HAVING A MID-LIFE CRISIS

Poems   LUISA A. IGLORIA

ISBN 978-1-927496-13-8

Cover art, design and editing by Elizabeth Adams

First Edition

Published by Phoenicia Publishing, Montreal
www.phoeniciapublishing.com

For my family, near and far.
For Brigid.

"The Buddha in me greets the Buddha in you."

"You are to travel far away.
What will you take with you?"
                    — The Dhammapada

CONTENTS

FOREWORD

The Buddha is Here, the Buddha is Everywhere, the Buddha is Nowhere

I look for him in my need, and over the years, I have needed. He is not an omniscient presence, not a deity, not watchful like the Christmastime Elf on the Shelf, reporting children's behavior—naughty or nice—to Santa. Sometimes I find him in unlikely places: hidden behind the Jesus statue in my neighbor's vegetable garden, in the closet of my childhood room to ward off the monster that comes out at night, on my shoulder whispering encouragement before entering awkward social gatherings. Sometimes he is a guide, Virgil to Dante. Sometimes an ear to receive my woes. Sometimes a voice—which either sounds like my Southside Chicago friends, tough and vulgar, or throaty and hoarse and speaking Thai like the monk who first taught me about the meaning of suffering. He takes on many forms. He can be transcendent, gold and without flaw. I might find him in a baseball cap and ripped jeans and a T-shirt. Or he can look like my mother and all I want to do is curl into him when I am despondent. He can be anywhere.

And now, I find him in the pages of this book.

Reading Luisa A. Igloria's poems is like opening doors within doors within doors. These doors give access to the mind, the imagination, into lush and lyric worlds. *The Buddha Wonders if She is Having a Mid-Life Crisis* continues pushing this space the poet occupies—a space between the real and the dream. And what a fantastical realm to exist in! I am lost. In a good way. I am taken. In a good way. But I am also found. Over and over again these poems find me. Over and over again I give over to them.

And then arrives the Buddha.

S/he possesses all that is human, every fragility we keep within. S/he is the voice we've locked inside. S/he is comprised of mythology, tradition, and imagination. Here the Buddha sits in a turbulent plane. Here s/he writes an advice column. Here s/he is the wallflower at a party overhearing a story about pot brownies. Igloria finds her Buddha in strange places too. But perhaps it is deeper. Perhaps the Buddha is the poet, and the poems are her doctrines layered in image and metaphor and meaning and meaninglessness. So Buddhist!

This is the beauty of this book. Nothing is what it seems. We are the sound grains of rice make in hollow bamboo; or we are whisked onto an operating table, floating off into a falsetto dream; or we are the drill during a dental procedure. Always we give way to the imagined state. Poem after poem reveals the Buddha. S/he is sneaky and coy. S/he peeks behind every stanza, meditating at every end-stopped line, her robes overflowing in every layer of images. And in the end, after we've taken in every poem, s/he finds a place in the center of us.

Ira Sukrungruang

January 12, 2018
Tampa, Florida

I

Perpetuum mobile

Bring a carrot or an apple
to the animal of the new year

that has come out of the gate,
that paws impatient at the pebbled

topsoil— Because it is ready
to canter into the field, offer it

a handful of blinding snow,
white as a portent for no sorrow,

cold as the slate which waits
to be turned into a track

where we'll walk forward
and back, into infinity.

The Buddha in me

        waves to the Buddha in you— Sometimes it
is the other way around. Mutually, we surprise
        each other, peering out suddenly from behind
a potted plant at a crowded mall, careening
        into a stack of trays at the cafeteria, or skidding
on a sidewalk sticky with rain and pollen
        so we have to help each other up. Sometimes
you've paid the fee at the toll before I even drive
        up to the window. Today, during my lunch break,
I crouched on the front steps of a building to scrape
        and pack snow into the shapes of birds: after the first
one, I made another, then another; until there were
        a dozen of them lined up with pebbles or bits of dirt
for eyes. The tops of their heads glistened in the sun.
        Most everyone rushed by, preoccupied. You
were the small one that shyly ventured out from behind
        your mother's market basket to ask if you could take
a snow bird into your cupped hands.

Mushi Ghazal

A scholar is being interviewed on the radio—
a fascinating account on in-dwelling insects.

She has studied insects and insect lore for many years
and is talking about Mushi, which in Japanese means insect.

There is also a manga with a character named Mushishi— shi means
teacher or doctor, and he has the ability to communicate with mushi.

It becomes clear that the scholar is talking not only about ants
or grasshoppers or bugs— your garden-variety insect—

but also about invisible or psychic bugs, the ones that determine how
you feel inside. According to Taoist stories: there is a resident insect

inside every human being. It seems there are at least four: living
in the head, in the trunk, in the legs. For every malaise, your insect

might be responsible. She reads a saying that translates
from Japanese: *My insect is in a good place*, or *My insect*

is in a bad place— therefore it is very important
to keep it happy, to take good care of your insect.

Raising your resident insect on a diet of mostly bile, salt,
and impure things may transform it into a monster-mushi

or demon. Legend says, there is one night every year
when it can climb out of the body, this demon-insect.

And then it can go to the gods to inform them of
your sins. Think twice then when you feel that insect-

like stirring inside: that quivering antenna of rage, the brittle
carapace of jealousy: don't let it out or do you in, your insect.

The Buddha is a wallflower

at most parties, but he does not mind at all.
He watches the couples on the dance floor twist
and shout or do the mashed potato, but he is
most content just drifting from one table island
to another, listening in on different conversations,
every now and then taking a sip from a glass
of very good Zinfandel or Riesling, nibbling
on a plate of hors d'oeuvres. At one of these
tables, the rheumatologist is trading stories
with his now grey-haired medical school buddies:
one night in particular, after a grueling week
of anatomy exams when they've all been invited
to a party and one of the first years brings
a tray of brownies "flavored" with weed—
Everyone's laughing again at how green he was,
popping square after square into his mouth until
the room began to spin, and all the people in it
loomed like a circle of trees around his head.
Even the most ravishing intern among them,
otherwise aloof and untouchable (the very one
the German student called "The Zexbomb"), stroked
his cheeks with great concern just before he
passed out on the couch. The Buddha marvels
when they speak of how, despite time and distance,
all this seems to have just happened. Even from
his seat on the periphery, he can see it, can
almost feel the long, cool fingertips brush against
his cheeks, his temples; how a memory not even his
can offer a spark undiminished by the years.

Rumor

Musk that soil gives off after rain,
first petrichor of approaching spring:

what message is written in the loam,
in the clustered weeds poised to send

tiny emissaries on the wind: death?
increase? In the window's embrasure

I pause to widen the in-between,

increased in the window's embrasure.
Tiny emissaries on the wind, death

in the clustered weeds poised to send
what message is written in the loam.

First petrichor of approaching spring,
musk that soil gives off after rain.

Five Mysteries

1

One clove of garlic swallowed whole to keep the heart valves open.
One tonic of vinegar and water to flush the throat.

Every morning before school she pinned a medallion over her chest,
upon the camisole. Breath was to eat and be kissed.

Teeth cracked open watermelon seeds, rows of disposable cathedrals.
In the smallest nave a lick of water, a slick of oil.

Pearl-like toes peeking out of orphanage cribs: her endless nightmare.
They found a way to let the child call her Mama; let her eat rice and fish
from her hands.

Moist ghosts wandering in the lung: mixture of camphor and boiling water.
Labor is the endless factory of the womb.

2

The father sits in the garden chair in his white undershirt and yellow bathrobe.
In the right-hand pocket, a Novena to the Infant Jesus of Prague; in the left, a nail-
clipper.

Night is falling. Or it is too early in the day. But the roosters are always crowing.
What is a truth? What is falsehood? What is merely unspoken or denied?

Blooms thinner than paper climb the outer walls.
Coming out of the alley, the street forks outward like a woman's thighs.

Place foxglove capsules under the tongue to order the fibrillations of the heart.
The hands have learned to press against the tops of the knees, thereby concealing
any agitation.

Meniscus: half a crescent under which a field of torsion suspends.
What is the first letter in your dictation, Father?

3

An oilcloth, an old rag; shreds from a raffia ribbon.
Imagine a living face, somewhere beneath the wooden surface.

Flour and salt, a leavening agent: all sift down, without a sound, into the bowl.
How little it takes to open a wound you didn't even think was there—

First sister, third brother, middle rung: every bird a wild card in the tree.
I live half an hour from the coast but the sea always knocks on the window.

Don't think you are not chosen. Don't think daylight falls only on certain
types of hair. Today, for instance: with its warm tendrils and grass-like movements,
its lucent swathe of mirrors.

I would want to be mummified in such bright blue air. In the wind-up tableau
two figures soldered to the base bow as if to take each other's leave.

4

Once I unzipped a dress embroidered with tulle flowers.
Once I lay in a bath of disappearing suds.

Is it possible to write aubades beginning with the words "I want?"
The hand sifts and measures: one weightlessness against another.

So much ambition has gathered with the dust of years.
Now I hunt the breath, the tutelage of empty space.

Bent twig, droopy flower, shallow basin of water: will you consider the triangle's
epistle? Heaven is generally 1 3/4 times the height and depth of the container. Man
is 3/4 of Heaven, Earth 3/4 of man in length.

In the milky light of morning, my shadow flickers on the sidewalk's slate.
Every stone sighs from its unchanging scripture.

5

Your hands beaded by rain.
Every softness: forged by fire, a blacksmith's tongs, the song of
a scudding hammer.

Small chamber in a stalk of green; your lip a liquid pause.
We are so careful not to startle the purple-headed bird.

When it is quiet I practice breathing like we did last.
I shut my eyes and enter the pool's blue membrane.

The sun's pulse turns, translucent cube in a highball.
When I rise I trail every wet strand of memory,

head tipped back to the vivid pull of wisteria—
Your mouth, your hands. A rivulet mercuries down the spine.

Never full, never empty—

the way fields look right after gleaning,
the way a city looks in the early hours
when at last the restaurants and pubs are closing
and the workers who have collected their tips
make their way to this place they know
(workers only) where you can get the red eye special,
chilaquiles, or caldo like someone's mama used to make
back in the day, coffee, eggs on toast with sriracha...

Never fevered, but always at a pitch,
the way the temperature of a body
that has known nothing but to be
in motion would melt the ice on the porch
just standing still. For such is the life
of the never here, never there, the ones
with such beautiful names, of course they come
from other worlds right here within our own—

Quarmaine, whose single rhinestone earring
chimes its light along with the cash register's
as he rings up the goods but pauses to ask:
*Wontons? I love wontons, like in the Chinese
takeout joints. How do you make that?*
And Ravi, who packs my groceries into a paper bag
listening as I list ingredients and make a motion
with my fingers, as though pulling the moist
corners of each square together into a kind of bud.

And I say drink the soup when it is scalding hot,
make lots of it to share— For it is always
never dark, or never light, or never something
or other enough, it is never good enough,
you are never going to be good enough
for whatever it is the jurors say it is
this time around, sitting in a circle like trees
that ring the frozen pond, their branches heavy
with the weight of all that sifted cold.

Ghazal, with Cow Burial

"There are only 31 horse burials in Britain and they are all with men."

Out of a pit, they've found a woman's bones— whittled by time,
bearded with dust, clutching the ambered remains of a cow.

Was she matriarch, widow, wife? Did she die struck by illness or blight?
Archeologists say her wealth and status are proven by this cow.

Some days, I quip to friends and family: my name might as well be
Bob (short for Beast of Burden). But life's yoke is heavier than a cow.

What would I want to take with me? In Chinese burials,
the dead are ferried to the afterlife: not on cows

but in paper limousines inked with symbols for wealth: coins, bills, sweets;
cigars, what one liked here enough to take to there; but not a cow—

In the winding Cordilleras I call home, the dead are neatly tucked among
the hills, with jars of betel nut and agate beads— never with a cow.

A friend reminds me: in Hindu myth, should the population
be in danger, they'll save the women, children, and their cows.

The cow that in this life was cow, does it remain the same? Does it dream
of feathered grass in the fields, of gnats, the low symphony of fellow cows

chewing their cud? They poke at beetles the color of jewels—
embellishment on face plates of sleeping mummies. The cow

as sacrifice, as plenty, as months of food and fat and solid warmth.
And the woman: how was she loved, missed, valued more than cow?

The Buddha fills in job applications

Almond the shape of my eyes; lotus
the width of my hips or the soft
inscrutability of a half-smile.
Virtue the act of sitting still,
going nowhere, being a stick-in-
the-mud. Or being pliable: sucking
the tummy in, filling it out with breath
or bread. Give me the bread, the bowl
of milk, honey from the hive, water
from the well, wine from the skin
that loosens all tongues and turns
every fool into a resident sage.

No, but where are you really from?

asks the khaki-clad man next to the Buddha
on the plane, sweeping an eye over his ash-
colored robe and knotted pantaloons, the single
strand of prayer beads around his neck that ends
in a tassel. He's already told him Sacramento,
but that he grew up in Houston then Virginia Beach,
and now he's on his way to a monastery in Korea
where he will spend a year in divinity studies
with other monks. *I can't place your accent,*
says his traveling companion who says his name
is Earl. *Thailand? The Philippines? You know I spent
close to eight years there, after my tour of duty
in 'Nam. Even went to school to use my benefits.
That's where I met my first wife. We lived in a whole
house we rented dirt cheap— less than a third
of what I'd have paid for an apartment back here.*
The Buddha is polite, only faintly smiling, saying
Is that so and *How interesting* at intervals. *And we
had a live-in maid and cook,* exclaims Earl—
*Oh, she was the best! I still dream of her
beef stews and noodles— Your people really
know what to do with food! And so industrious,
always cleaning, morning till night!* The Buddha
keeps a smile on his face, though part of him really
wants to roll his eyes and say something.
Fortunately, the pilot comes on the PA system
to say they are entering an area of turbulence
and should re-fasten their seat belts and push
back their tray tables. When the plane swings
like a tin pail in a roiling wind, the Buddha
closes his eyes, folds his palms together
in his lap, and begins to chant very softly under
his breath *Nam-myoho-renge-kyo.* Earl says,
*Whatever that is, little bro, I hope it means Hurry up
get us home and out of this soup in one piece.*

Interpellated

We sit in the grass having come nearly late.
We've made our way under the trees, rough

ground cover prickling at our sandaled heels.
The moon is a wafer split exactly in half.

Someone asks, *If only one part of the balance
is visible, should we assume the other unseen*

is properly accounted for? If you haven't
been where we've been, it's difficult

to understand what it's really like.
Sure, the streets are spotless and the hedges

well-manicured. In this part of town,
the doors of townhouses all have beautiful,

ornate knockers, polished to such a high shine.
But who told you the trees bear only fruits

of gold? I and my kind walk beneath endless
rows of them, stretching our shirts and aprons

to catch what careless afterthought the unseen gods
might lob out their windows. We hold up our heads

and smile at those we meet. We carry laminated plastic
cards with which we provision time, our little dignities.

The last temple in the north

Run away from all that postmodern theory and complexity, its dense linguistic curtains, its smoke and mirrors; those parables about the emptiness at the heart of the onion, the scintillating space in that final temple more alabaster than an egg or the Taj Mahal where nothing can live, not even love, not even poetry... Once we understand we have nothing, then and only then can we approach poetry. And I was merely a girl from the highlands, a girl from a town on an old ivory map so far away in the hills, too difficult to climb through limestone canyons... So the friars simply said *Hija de puta, there is no one there to count in our census, ergo it does not exist*— Where they did not persist, others did. Look at our archives of poems in the shape of our enemies' severed heads. Look at our feathered amulets, our chest plates studded with silence after silence, deconstructed into fearful significance.

Absence, Presence

Every absence is an ancestor: speak to it,
ignore it, feed it, turn it out of doors,
it will not matter— It knows where you live,
which side of the pillow you prefer in sleep,
where you buy your eggs and milk and toilet
paper. It knows whom you last kissed on the mouth,
how you cried to read that poem written by
your daughter, your bewilderment at the stroke
after stroke of bad luck that came the year
you decided to say I do to your green, unproven
heart. The roses in the garden bloomed and withered,
and then came back. *Dormant* doesn't mean dead,
only sleeping. Winter is another form of absence,
some say a kindness: substituting white
after white for all the gutted fields before
their softening in spring. Absence, presence—
I bow to you my ancestors; I stoke the fire
and save the bones for soup in these cold months
when I am most reminded I am your kin.

Cameos

Unpacking boxes, I kept finding creased prayer cards to various saints.
Who are you? I asked of one indecipherable face on paper
soft as chamois— part bird, part woman, mouth open as if in song.

La novelista said she knew she was almost done when she went
through chapters like a cleaning lady might walk from room to room
polishing every surface, even the hinges of the candelabra.

My mother announced she had a sudden craving for roast chestnuts.
*Should I buy a ticket to Germany, she wondered aloud, and travel
through all the towns I can find starting with "H?"*

One wall a dark orange, the others an odd layering
of pink and blue. A red gate, a water tank raised
on a metal frame. Curtains of printed oilcloth.

What you imagine betrays you
to the photograph. In life as in literature, the frame
cannot be more ornate than the image warrants.

This remains: memory of a field of waving grasses.
Where were you going? Where were you taking me?
Night and its salty fragrance carried by wind.

How Much

The Buddha looks at items on display
at the duty-free shop in the airport,
where he is waiting for his connecting flight:
rows of Swiss and Belgian chocolate; Courvoisier,
champagnes Moët & Chandon, Dom Perignon;
perfume from French designer houses— A sales
attendant with a silk scarf knotted tastefully
around her neck approaches, waving a tester
and a little paper wand: *Would you like to sample*
the latest spring floral, with musk notes
and a spicy vanilla top that dries to a light
jasmine finish? This unexpected recital
sounds almost intimate though he knows it isn't.
The problem with trying to be in the world
while not being caught up by it is that one *is*
always in the world. Despite himself he blushes,
feels a damp sweat film his underarms. A cloud
of expensive fragrance arises and for a moment
he wishes there was someone waiting to receive
just such an offering from his feverish hands
upon his return— for whom he might say
to the sales clerk *Wrap it up*, without
bothering to look at the price tag.

Transplanting

You have no shovel, so you forage in the cupboards
to find only a plastic fork and two knives.
Is this what it feels like in those fairy tales
where the girl is sentenced to labor after impossible
labor, before being granted access and social mobility?
What the villain/ess doesn't understand: the girl
was born in a third world country, where she learned
to shampoo and bathe with a scant pailful of water,
where snacks are a euphemism for all the inventive
ways one might use every part of the animal for food.
Stables, lions, sky-darkening hordes of birds—
A deus ex machina, just another name
for cheating. Your parents have to work
in the fields. Or they are sick, missing, dead.
Try dandling your new baby brother on one
hip while feeding your two-year old sister
when you're only five. Take them out
into the avenue to weave through traffic, splay
begging fingers against the tinted window glass
of cars. Shred after shred layers the years;
petulance and bad temper are so unnecessary.
They will not make the miracle you pray for—
only stubborn patience, the work of your hands
as you make a hollow in the gravelly soil deep enough
for this plant you have brought to take root and grow.

Hollowed

I like the sound of rice or bits of gravel falling through a cylinder of bamboo.
I like the way this dry rain falls in the vertical hollow of this space.

The rushing sound resembles water and is pleasing to the ear; it's possible
to slow the grains' descent with obstacles thrust at intervals within the tube.

On the bare arm, on the shoulder, on the back: the *mambabatok* taps with inked
needle and a mallet the figure for mountain, almost identical to water.

High above the Pacific, a hurricane whirls like a monstrous flower—
In its center is a cup where all the moisture in the world has thinned

to the sound of stacked bracelets. In the highlands where we lived,
the women fasten hawk bells to the ends of belts; and on their palms,

clap a devil-chaser. When they walk at dusk from the fields, the sound makes
a small nimbus— matter struck on matter, penetrating the spirit world.

The Buddha wonders if she is having a mid-life crisis:

these days, tears come easily and often, in public, at
inappropriate times; or without preamble as she drives
the car to or from work. Sometimes she has to pull up
by the curb to wipe waterfalls from her eyes— she doesn't
want to ruin her spotless driving record, much less cause
injury to another creature on the road. *Ask your doctor*
about hormone replacement therapy, says her girlfriend.
Maybe get your thyroid checked, says another. *Nothing*
wine can't cure. Or a vacation. Plus mani-pedi and a Thai
massage: those are the best! A full Thai massage session
typically lasts two hours. Someone walks up and down
the length of your back and cracks your knuckles, pulls
your fingers, toes, and ears, rotates your arms and legs
and kneads your skin until it glows. The Buddha tries
to remember the last time she glowed, when anyone said
she looked good in whatever kind of light, when the lines
around her eyes laughed then turned into quilled
ribbons at the ends— A long time. In college,
she'd read about the paradox of motion: how that
which is in locomotion must arrive at the half-way stage
before it arrives at the goal— She remembers thinking
then, as she does now, how this was either the smartest way
to talk oneself into tackling daunting goals and distances
in manageable increments, or the dumbest reason
for staying home since any progress was doomed
to impossibility from the start. And in the case of this
potential mid-life crisis, the middle is the middle
of the middle of the middle from the moment
anybody ever took their first breath here.

The Buddha goes on the Internet

to look for a licensed counselor and therapist
and finds a practice in a street next to
the drugstore where he fills his prescriptions.
From among the photos on the website, he decides
on the one who looks the kindest: a woman with chestnut
hair and an old-fashioned first name. She's not really
smiling in the photograph but her eyes are. He picks up
the phone and makes an appointment for Tuesday after next...
What? You don't think this is a plausible story? You think
the Buddha has no need to work out issues, or even that
he has any issues? This is partly the problem— all
the press he's ever gotten has him just about perfected.
Every brass likeness and stone statue, from museum gallery
to the home improvement section of Lowe's or Home Depot,
depicts him in nothing but an attitude of pure serenity
even if next to him there is an entire box of manic-
looking garden gnomes— Thumb lightly touching index
finger in the Gyan Mudra, eyes two perfect almonds
resting on the calm lake of his face, who would think
he has any need to unburden himself and his domestic woes
to another? It's not easy to think of the ideal as less
than ideal, of the one who serves as poster child
having the same capacity for hurt and need that we all do.
So then, whatever you believe, be gentle with the ones
who've listened through the years and asked how they
could take away some of your suffering, the ones
who sat you down and showed you how to breathe in
then exhale slowly, one nostril at a time; the ones
who patiently collected your tears in bottles smaller
than your little finger and showed you how they
could turn into something else if you laid them
lovingly on the sill and gave them a chance to dry.

You seem to be carrying a lot of guilt,

the therapist says to the Buddha ten minutes
into her first session. She sighs, tentatively massaging
the sides of the stress ball she has been given.

Is it that obvious? she asks, even if she knows
the answer. She thought she was doing a pretty good job
sitting still, holding her fears and anxieties in her mind

without judging, without undue attachment, without blame
— well, ok, trying. It is so difficult for the heart to be
in more than one place at any given time, more

if you are a mother: every hurt hurts, every flutter
ravages the surface on which the days must progress
with their sometimes terrible banality, with their small

and therefore acute reprieves of joy. Meanwhile, the hours
spread like a cowl, like the shadow of a cobra sitting
just a hand-span away, its breath the breath of the eternal

that all these years had passed mistakenly as mere
nagging: parent hovering impatient in the doorway,
gardener bent over a tray of new seeds; bird nudging
the fledgling closer to the end of the branch.

The therapist explains to the Buddha

the concept and effects of "Catastrophizing"
using references to Chicken Little, Pooh
Bear, Wile E. Coyote, and The Roadrunner.

He understands everything perfectly in his mind,
having had many occasions to dispense similar advice
to others through the years. Nonetheless he is charmed
by this new cast of colorful characters and how they

play out one worst case scenario after another—
*There is a crack in the ceiling of heaven! The sky
is falling! There is a raincloud growing larger above
my head!* He likes when the therapist explains

that the honey-colored bear with the ample belly
resembling his in some art works is our baseline condition:
at rest, without stress, comfortable and at ease in the wood
of the world. But the agitated chicken, the wound-up coyote

and the perennially ruffled bird are ready
not only to leap on the first train of worry, but also
to ride the same crooked track that has gouged itself
so deep into the landscape it has no other

destination but down. *Just stay on the platform,*
says the therapist whose first name in Welsh
means pure-hearted: *Not so fast. Let's make a list
of why your world right now is not about to end.*

Five Worry Beads

This is for the whites of eggs I failed to coax
to airiness, so they puddled at the bottom of the bowl

This is for the ring of silver I was given
but lost one day in a shower stall at the gym

This is for the gate I thoughtlessly let swing, that hit
the child traipsing behind full on the forehead

This is for the years that stretched like doors
in a dream hallway, so you couldn't hear my voice

This is for the compass rose that turned and the weather
vane that tilted when I opened my arms to embrace the wind

Stone

Stone of petty accusation, stone that rolls
from year to year increasing in volume
and dumb heft— You do not look good
in the garden. You do not look good,
not even as a paperweight.

II

Florescent

Full-blown, blowsy: blooms that used to be
mere hints on the tips of trees—

Overnight it has become spring, season of
wild and ruddy burgeoning. They move too rapidly

into their prime, trying on dress after dress,
discarding cardigans, pinning on costume jewelry.

Perfume on wrists, blushed cheeks. Dark
consigned to evenings. Make pretty; kiss kiss!
Perfume on wrists, blushed cheeks. Dark

discarding cardigans. Pinning on costume jewelry
into their prime, trying on dress after dress.

Wild and ruddy burgeoning. They move too rapidly
overnight— it has become spring, season of

mere hints on the tips of trees;
full-blown, blowsy, blooms that used to be.

The Buddha listens

in the kitchen to a classical program
on the radio one evening while cold rain lashes
the window before turning into pellets of ice—
And he thinks Mendelssohn's Octet in E flat
Major, Op. 20 is the perfect soundtrack for this
moment— the violins and their upbow so quickly
spanning and gathering a range of feeling
he did not know still simmered under his skin.
Where did they come from: that flare of resentment,
that thorn of anger, the ache of loneliness
from a love he yearned for but could not have?
How is it possible to cultivate detachment
at the same time that one practices compassion?
He rinses his cup and saucer and sets them
on the rack to dry, his fingers lingering
in midair as if to trace the notes
that exit in the scherzo.

Who was your first love?

  a first grader asks the Buddha in the informal Q & A
at the elementary school where he is making a visit.
The homeroom teacher turns to admonish this foolishness
and a ripple of laughter goes through the audience,
but the Buddha raises his hand gently and smiles at the boy.
The question has brought him back not to the day of his betrothal
nor even to his wedding, but to a brief moment one morning—
After long illness and sleepless nights fraught with care
and worry, how he and his love held each other in the middle
of the room, not raked by tumultuous desire, not grasping;
eyes speaking, just breathing. Who was the first to break
the silence, to say *May we be blessed to live longer
with each other?* For everything is a gift, he says
to the gathering: the first phoebe of spring, a torn
strip of clothing that reddens the branch on which
it has caught; the face light etches on a plate of metal
looking back at you at last, as if it had traveled
an eternity just to give you this greeting, this welcome.

How long can you sit still

in one place, not blinking, not twitching, not scratching
an itch on the far side of your back, not even to shield
with a broad leaf from the peepal tree your face from the sun?
How long can you suffer the noise of passing rickshaws,
jeering children, the ungainly parade of goats and cattle,
quizzical stares from passersby, the village simpleton's
dropped jaw from wondering in a brief moment of lucidity
if his place of honor has just been usurped? And how long
can you listen past the drone of dragonflies and the chorus
of frogs at night, during the day the swish of scythes
in unison moving across the fields for reaping? The well
of silence is long and deep and full of echoes.
Birds fly across the opening, where the sky is framed
as through a porthole in a ship, a piece of glass
at the end of a long telescope. Rain, twigs, and stones
drop unseen into its depths, and it is difficult to hear
how long it takes each of them to reach the mossy bottom.

Salutation

My heart bows to the field streaked
by the sun's rare currency this morning

to the worries that call my name
over and over like I am their favorite child

to the ridiculous kindness
of the wild turkeys' chatter

to you who've called
me stranger, friend, lover

to you who've sung me to sleep
and kissed me in doorways

to you who've made space
for me on this window-ledge of words—

And you on the edge of the field, I bow to you
all in shadow, your patience outlasting us all

This bead

        I finger all
                night long, this bone
made smooth from constant
        plying; these drops
                that fall down the gradated
steps of the motorized
        tabletop fountain
                before they climb up again;
January's recycled sorrows
        come to haunt the mind in April,
                these prayer flags that flutter
squares of color in uneven wind.

Going under the gamma knife,

first he's slipped under a veil of ether —layman's
approximation of what happens when the right

dose of anesthetic is delivered, in order for
the team of neurosurgeons (plus one physicist)
to attach a lightweight frame to his skull.

Of course, before this happens, they explain
the details: showing him the clear spherical frame
with its four metal pins they will fix in place

(two at his temples, two in the back
of his head), converging points through which
controlled beams of radiation will travel

to their target: a nerve at the bottom of
the brain stem. The smiling nurse takes his pulse
and blood pressure, hooks him up to the IV drip, asks

if he has any questions. He knows that stereotactic
refers to surgical techniques involving the accurate
positioning of probes inside the brain or other

parts of the body. By this time he is drowsy,
drifting in and out of a kind of twilight zone
but conscious enough to respond when prodded.

He hears but doesn't see the instruments
dropped back on the covered trays;
he feels them wheel the gurney through

the double doors, slide his body into place
beneath the machine. *This will take just
a little under an hour*, says the nurse,

*but we have a Pandora station. What kind of music
do you like?* He remembers telling her The Police
or Sting, and then hearing The BeeGees' unmistakable

falsetto rendition of "Staying Alive" just before a clear voice
tells him the treatment's over, they're bringing him back
to recovery, to check and monitor vital signs.

Innervate

Innervate: in·ner·vate / i' nər ̩vāt
verb; anatomy, zoology; to supply
(an organ or other body part)
with nerves.

Researching *tic douloureux*, I click
on a related link and learn The International
Headache Society is not the sort of organization
where fellow sufferers of the migraine

and its lesser varieties come together annually
at a convention center in Cancun or the Pyrenees,
to dine and drink while documenting and celebrating
their accomplishments of pain. But it is the IHS

we must thank for the classification system
now most widely employed for headaches:
a generous umbrella under whose awning
you'll find everything from tension headaches

with or without aura and light sensitivity,
to cluster headaches accompanied by drooping
eyelids, nausea, runny noses, throbbing temples;
or primary stabbing headaches like ice picks

to the brain, and hemicrania continua,
delivering continuous unilateral pain. The brain,
however— little hilly village criss-crossed
by winding trails and nestled like an egg

in a walled-in fortress— is not itself
sensitive to pain. The brain has no pain
receptors, as so clearly illustrated in that
famous scene from the movie "Hannibal,"

where Lecter removes the top of Krendler's skull,
then scoops up some prefrontal cortex to sauté
presumably in butter and garlic with a splash
of white wine before he feeds it to

the unsuspecting one. From a page in an early
edition of *Gray's Anatomy*, the pathway
of cranial nerves branching through and around
the brain stem is a complicated multi-lane

highway. Who can even keep up with the varied
streams of information traveling at high speeds,
much less police their frenzied signaling
as they cross from one lane to another?

The ancients thought that headaches
and convulsive fits were the work of evil
spirits, and Neolithic fossils provide
evidence of practices for releasing

these demons— including trepanation
(drilling a hole or removing a section
of the skull). Still, despite our intricate
science and the rays of radiation we fire

with focused precision at a vessel lodged deep
in the body's recesses, then and now the mystery
of pain remains arcane as that of pleasure, as that
most final pair of mysteries, life and death—

And since this is so, why not heed what the Ebers
Papyrus (Egypt, 1200 BC) instructs about the latter:
how *half an onion and the froth of beer are*
considered a delightful remedy against death.

Cascade

What I want is immediacy, the nub
of the moment pressed without doubt
into my side, the tremor that comes
sometimes before sight, before taste
or touch. Whatever might be lost, don't
take that away from me: stars pouring
out of the firmament, not ever holding
back the flood over my small ladle.

III

The Buddha tells his parents

he is dropping out, leaving everything behind, going out into *the real world* to see
what it's like there. *Are you mad?* screams his mother. *Who do you think you are,* his
father yells, shaking a fist in his face— *A freaking hippie from America?* They go
on like this for at least a few hours, pleading, cajoling, wringing their hands and
pacing back and forth across the great hall of the ancestral home until their skin oils
deepen the sheen of the wood floor. Henceforth, the servants will never again need
polish it. The Buddha does not change his mind. One thing you must know: he has
always been like that since childhood— once he decides something, there's usually
no way to turn it around. He packs a few simple articles of clothing and a wooden
bowl, the sight of which fills his mother with such dread she begins to wail. *Take
a pair of sandals at least,* she sobs. *Your feet, that never so much as walked a block of
pavement in all your life!* But now the stones of the world will cut open the skin of
his beautiful feet, the mud and dirt change their color. He knows and yet does not
know what else is coming. The new life is already walking down to the garden gate,
lifting the latch, turning its face to the countryside and to the great meditation on
what lies beyond.

Blessing

A rain of ink fell on a clear day and I was refreshed by its lightly lightly double syllables; and it made me think, dearest dearest one of how we are all fussy birds with too many feathers; but a little water will not do any harm. Aren't we all imprisoned in bad translations, wanting to escape— brides shedding our tulle and crinoline to run off with a rogue? My most cherished and crucial here and now, you are present as time and as gift, even in the boundaries where most of us dwell, every kind of hybrid, little cutting grafted from another vine. Seasonal as migrant labor, temporal as weather. Wild birds, untethered on yellow bicycles or riding in cabs driven through unfamiliar cities by immigrants born in another clime. In the rear-view mirror, my Ethiopian driver Beni-yamin cocks one eyebrow at my backpack and says, *Lady, but where is your luggage for putting in the trunk?* And I laugh and say *There is only this.* He tells me of his mother who went away to work for a family in the city when she was only ten. From the glass his eyes look back at mine. Beni-yamin, Benjamin, he is only twenty-four. And he is telling me I have to go back someday and buy a house to which I can return when the rain does not fall so softly softly anymore. What if that kind of rain is everywhere? It will not be enough to find the clay that matches. *May you have a good life*, he says. The words, the words might be one place to start.

Preguntas

Who will sift the snow fine as dust
from the eyes of the clock

Who will find the ring
buried in layers of cake

How does the tendril on the vine
still believe in the rotary phone

Who will take off his shoes
to walk across the blistered sand

When will the child lay a hand
across the mouth of suffering

Why is the rooster's crow
indifferent to the progress of snails

Why should I return
dreams that refuse to open

Who will instruct
a wounded star

Who will embroider the cave
with splendid suns

What is required for you
to take up a weed and dance

Unending Lyric

Zealous at long rehearsals, tenacious at audition— the brushed
      yellow-olive, drab-coated vireo hangs upside down then
exits the tree with a prize: red berry or dun kernel, blur of
      winged insect disappearing down the hatch of its throat.
Valediction isn't its song: not a saying farewell, not the
      up-swelling notes of a soprano— just the same
tremulous question and answer all through the day.
      Sound shivers like a string when plucked. I learned
rote-singing, then followed the pencil across the staff:
      quarter-notes, eighths, sixteenths; the rests like little
puffs of breath propelling onward. And yes it's work,
      opening the chest to let the air of longing out for that
nimbus of release, though brief and incommensurate.
      My audible heart wants a nest like a cup in the fork of a tree.
Lit up at night, in that forest of softened trills, who
      knows how the air might shear its stuttering refrains,
join the failed parts of songs as leitmotif?
      I practice and practice though nobody hears.
Hoarse from effort and nearly at empty, I
      gloss sometimes over difficult parts that
find a way of coming back, sliding into another
      edge of passage. Nothing ever stays still:
do you see how the moon shimmers, then
      clears a path for the screech owl's call?
Bright, brassy, or somber rounding in the mouth—
      answer that burns salt shapes on the tongue.

The Buddha wanders into the wilderness

that is the downtown mall, and enters
a cookery store to look for an inexpensive
Dutch oven wherein he might attempt
to recreate his mother's boeuf bourguignon,
slow-simmered and rich with the flavor of beef
braised in red wine, caramelized onions,
garlic, bacon, mushrooms, and a bouquet
garni. Looking through a shelf of enamel-
glazed French cast iron casseroles and
surreptitiously fingering the three-digit
price tags, he is hailed by a sales clerk
with a bountiful head of curls. Her name
tag reads "Artemis," and she offers
little paper cup samples of flavored coffee
brewed from individual pods dropped in a chrome-
fitted machine vaguely resembling a tabletop
silo. He restrains himself from asking
where her hunting dogs are, and her fierce
handmaidens; and how it has come to pass
that she has wound up in this sad position
instead of calling the shots in the glade,
ordering a wall of bristling spears raised
around the sacred pool in which she bathes…
Instead he bows and takes the proffered sip,
thanks her, and decides: rather than meat,
he will have something raw and fresh
for dinner— perhaps a salad of greens
with slices of crisp, tart fruit; nothing
animal that might have writhed in
the agony of the chase before the kill.

Because of global warming,

the Ladies of the Monday Afternoon Club
have started a clothing drive for the Buddha,
who continues his travels abroad in a world with more
and more unpredictable weather, garbed in the same outfit
he has worn for who knows how many centuries now:
thin pantaloons and a cotton robe of ochre, to be
in some minimum conformity while fulfilling the life
of an ascetic. He probably wears a men's size 8 shoe,
as evidenced by the shape of his *pada* in stone:
high arches, broad heels, beautiful toes and ankles
(according to *The 80 minor characteristics
of the Buddha* in the *Āgamas*). The good Ladies
are worried he will take cold walking through prairies
once gold with wheat and now festooned with ice,
along the coast where fine sand beaches are now
unseasonably powdered with snow. His late mother
the queen would know the value of a nice care package;
after all, didn't she suffer goring in the side
by a six-tusked elephant in order for him to be conceived?
No matter that our children are grown, no matter that they
are the Buddha, no matter that they brush the dust of home
off their sandals and leave to make their own way— we want
to do whatever we can for our young to be warm and safe
in this strange and sometimes inhospitable universe.

Traveling Mercies

And when long
winter breaks

at last, I pray
I will remember

how on my way
I stop to finger

nubs pressing their
blind shapes, one

after the other,
through the heart.

The Buddha considers with all seriousness

the variety of decisions that revolve around desire:
Nutella chocolate chip with sea salt, pistachio lemon
creme, or cinnamon amaretto swirl? Where is human nature
so weak as in the ice cream section of a 24-hour grocery store?
And really, this is just the tip of the proverbial iceberg,
only one layer of this rainbow-shingled world shiny with neon
and digital contraptions, sprinkled with add-ons. He is tempted
to pack up his new digs and tell his young family
they're moving to the country, to an island in Micronesia,
somewhere they can hang laundry to dry on the line, collect rain
water in barrels, plant their own tomatoes, squash, and bitter
melons, send the kids to school and watch them walk down
the dirt path in flip-flops without worrying about
their safety— But he's promised his wife he'll try
to find a way to live in the humid armpit of the city,
practice what he's always talking about: simplify,
let go, right where it is. And *right where it is*
is right here, right now: even in this small,
frozen section of the universe, where desire after desire
jostles for attention— blackberry cobbler, peaches
and cream, orange Creamsicle, black walnut crunch—
Each a hymn to the impossibility of satisfaction, reverie
that purchase promises but might not in the end provide.

The Buddha sits at a communal table sipping Prosecco

from a mason jar instead of any of a number of craft
beers on the drinks menu. She is eating her topless
brisket sandwich with melted honey chipotle cheddar
and arugula (which is a tasty, updated version
of the standard open face beef and cheddar melt
she might have had in her youth), and she wonders
if she and her date might be the oldest persons
in the room— It's a Saturday night and the restaurant,
a refurbished factory space with open rafters
and a wall which opens like a garage door to let in
the cooling breeze, is packed with people in their 20s
and 30s wearing vintage and thrift store fashions,
distressed jeans, old-school sneakers, edgy
hairstyles. The music playing from the back
is probably by an indie band; the volume's a little
too loud for her taste, and not at all conducive
to the kinds of sensitive, intelligent, and culturally
aware conversations which should be taking place
in every corner of this kind of establishment, according
to the demographic. But the food is very good, and so is
the wine; and no one looks at her and her grey-haired
partner as if to appraise whether they are representatives
of mainstream elite, conservative, conformist, or consumer
culture. Her date adjusts his thick-rimmed glasses, leaning
close to get her attention. He points to the tapas bar across
the street and the window of a third-floor apartment, at which
a large black dog's ensconced, as if surveying the scene below.
Look how the animal's above us all, he says; how effort-
lessly it keeps its cool, how uninflected by deliberate irony,
how uninfluenced by everything we work so hard to resist
but give ourselves to and that eventually swallows us whole.

What would the Buddha say

if he discovered his teenage son
had an Internet addiction? Would he storm
into his room and pull by the wire

every electronic gadget snaking from the wall
outlets, cast them out of the garden of innocent
childhood transformed overnight into a landscape
charged with hormones and other such land mines

and say *You, you are grounded for all eternity?*
How would he sit on the sage-green cushions
to deliver with utmost patience
that famous lecture on how everything—

despite the shimmer of advertising—
is illusion, if the young acolyte
had earphones on and the music drowned out
his father's even, reasonable tones?

The thing I want to say
is that the Buddha was also human—
except perhaps with an extraordinary
capacity for understanding I do not yet

but would so dearly like to have.
The other thing I wonder about is how long
it would take to arrive at the doorstep of such
unwavering equanimity when it seems

it is either the day of the great deluge
or the hour just after the waters have finally
receded; but there, at the horizon,
is a glimpse of yet another rising wave—

The Buddha subs for a weekly advice columnist

Dear Buddha,
                    I was in the middle
of my patient's root canal procedure,
when a glint of sunlight ricocheted off
the mouth mirror and struck me in the eye;
all I could think of was *How many more*
of these do I need to do before I can finalize
my divorce, ditch my horrible in-laws and the SOBs
pretending to be my golf buddies, and start anew?
Why did I let myself be bullied by my parents into this
career in endodontics, instead of following in your
footsteps? Also, I am losing my hair and wonder if
you have any advice on shaving it all off at one time.
Yours truly, Middle Aged and Unhappy in Florida.

Dear Middle Aged and Unhappy in Florida,
                                        yours truly
would have no real advice on shaving it all off at one time.
My decision had more to do with trying to travel more lightly.
I know what you mean about parents who come on too strong:
but we have to believe they only want the best for us, even when
they misguidedly think the pinnacle of success is membership
at a country club with a golf course, among other things.
As for your wife and in-laws, I do not know the circumstances
that placed them in your life and you in theirs; one must
always inquire, what are we asked to learn from each other?
This much I believe: the things we think and do attract
our fate, though they are in the end illusion.
When insight strikes like a too-bright reflection
or a vehicle's high-beam lights, the first instinct is often
to freeze and recoil. Afterward comes the adjustment,
the much more unpleasant task of tunneling anew
into the self, digging for the root of things.

The Buddha remembers Miss Sifora Fang,

his third grade teacher from years ago: diminutive
terror of the daily twenty-item spelling quiz, bespectacled,
hair pulled always into a severe chignon— How she parsed

sentences across three panels of chalkboard, lectured on
the solidity of nouns and verbs and the relative shiftiness
of adverbs. Therefore, when he reads *the half-leafed-out lilac
seems to glow, achingly green against the brown woods,*

his mind begins to revise: is it *achingly, the half-leafed-out lilac
seems to glow green,* or is it *the half-leafed-out lilac seems
to glow a painful shade of green?* He suspects Miss Sifora Fang
would not approve. Likely, she would interrogate the very lilac

by the garden gate as to its blushing intentions, and certainly
the speaker as to why the sight of light striking the undersides
of leaves should stir a wound. Once, she sternly asked
the Buddha: *Why are you crying?* as he struggled to find

the right words for a difficult lesson. *To be precise*
does not necessitate complication, except that it is so
difficult to pluck the right thoughts from the always moving
branch, and find the words to flesh out what it is they mean.

The Buddha doesn't give a damn

You look so beautiful, at peace
and in your own spirit, says a friend
whom the Buddha has not seen in a while.
She beams and hugs her back, while mentally
reminding herself to check in the mirror
for what might have spurred this
compliment. Her hair is loosely pinned up
because of the humidity; she's in dark-
colored jeans, a t-shirt, a faded cardigan
even on a workday, just because comfort
now comes first. Every so often, on special
occasions, she'll wear a dress and heels,
put on some makeup— foundation, eye
shadow, lipstick, but no mascara. Now
that she's past 50, she finally knows
what it means to not give a damn: to be
unbothered by the decision to not go out
drinking with students; to eat breakfast
for dinner and dessert for breakfast. She is
nonplussed when a wind lofts her skirt above
her knees, when a rolling wave slaps down
the top of her strapless swimsuit at the public
beach. She simply tugs the offending
garment back in place, shrugs, carries on.

The Buddha picks up a call without first checking caller ID,

so he is unprepared for the phone sales person's smooth
segue from the opening "Do I have the pleasure of speaking
with Mr. Buddha?" to a series of personal-seeming questions.
Too late, he realizes these are geared toward selling him
a life insurance product. But, having nothing more pressing
to do than water his dendrobiums and clean the bathroom
before a simple supper and his bedtime medication,
he lets the agent who identifies himself as "Joe"
work through his spiel. The Buddha answers in good
faith questions about dependents and beneficiaries:
No one, and everyone; and whether he might appreciate
the difference between a simple term life insurance
versus a universal or whole-life policy which combines
life coverage with an investment fund: *The goal*
of all life is the movement toward greater and
greater enlightenment, which is the freedom at last
from suffering and illusion. Joe the agent splutters,
fumbles to pick up the thread, then falls momentarily
silent before concluding he is speaking with a madman.
Therefore, when he disconnects, he does not hear
the Buddha's questions: *What good is the cash value*
one might build from investments made by the company
in my imperfect life? and *Even if there is no deductible*
because death is a one-time event— from every iteration
of suffering, do we not die repeatedly and wither
faster than thistles under the scorching sun?

Exquisite

Open wide, says the dentist's assistant.
I'm going to stretch your mouth a little bit more,
ok? She blinks at the overhead light; the xylocaine
with the bitter bubblegum taste and scent
has taken effect, and the dentist plunges
the tip of the needle into her lower gum
and jawline, pulling at her cheek for effect.
When the drill begins to widen the broken
enamel of her tooth to prepare for its filling,
she closes her eyes and tries to pretend
she is on a lounge chair poolside, and
the noise and discomfort are merely effects
of a nearby construction project. She's marveled
at small glimpses caught in the mouth mirror,
her jagged teeth miniature rows of mountains
receding in a ridged landscape. She remembers
a black-and-white film she watched long ago:
"The Passion of Joan of Arc," how she found it
impossible to tell whether it was rapture
or suffering that crossed the stark face
of the girl martyr played by Maria Falconetti;
how the tipped-back head, wide eyes, and parted
lips might signify both agony and the most
exquisite pleasure. And she can see it's true
from the faces of people buckled into their seats
as the roller coaster picks up speed before
the plunge, from the way the lovers writhing
in the sheets approach their climax: how thin
the line that separates one state from
another, how quickly pain might transition
to the joy of release then back again.

The Buddha walks a mile

in her shoes at the local community college
for Women's History Month. With the other men
who signed up for the event, he rummages through boxes
of women's shoes looking for a pair that will fit.
You want socks with those, bro? asks the office
assistant, as he gingerly slips on a pair of open-toe
leopard print wedge platforms. He wiggles his foot around
a couple of times before he can slip it in; his bunion
always gives him trouble. They're getting ready to walk
around the quad, past the student dorms and down
to the plaza in the middle of the mall, where a SAFE
counselor will hand out pamphlets with statistics
on how many women on college campuses get raped,
assaulted, victimized in domestic relationships.
The Buddha is disturbed by these stories. He cannot
fathom the hatred and the violence, the displaced
self-loathing that seeks its target in female
bodies, the suffering. He recalls the brothels
along the coast, the sad eyes of women in the windows;
the way, in his own hometown, there are still fathers
who think daughters don't need to go to school,
households where girls are made to take their sleeping
pallet outside to the porch or behind the kitchen
when they have their period. He hitches his robe
a little higher around his ankles; he adjusts
his stride, determined not to wobble or fall.

True Meridian

Where I wanted to go, years ago, seemed so far away:
a dream, a fantasy even, in the blue distance.

Not now what might be purchased, what comes with
a ticket, that place of no return in the blue distance.

All that glitters isn't a rhinestone seam on a fishnet
stocking: the long hallway beckons in the blue distance.

And the hills will be there, but that city to which
you dedicate songs has receded in the blue distance.

This is the way it is for exiles, for poets, for lovers
who want to keep something pure in the blue distance.

For instance: that parapet where you leant as a child
to watch boats in the harbor, in the blue distance.

Spirits distilled from the lowly potato, the unassuming
birch: waters that have traveled from a blue distance.

Have you changed? and how? ask compatriots. What they mean,
really, is: *Have I also traversed the same blue distance?*

On the eve of the lunar year I walked about with a saucer of salt,
a handful of augurs— Talismans to ground me in this blue distance.

CODA

Keep me

from turning into a particle of disbelief: so many of them, each a universe where
things pretend to be what they are only to spite themselves— milk in the jug never
sweet, the cream always on the verge of curdling; a downspout refusing anything
that might resemble water. Oh how miserable to maintain such a charade, the
stream only doubling back on itself because it must disprove what some philosopher
said about not being able to step in the same current twice. Keep me from the old
shell game of anxiety, guessing which tin holds the crystal paperweight and which
the red bean we will boil for supper. Instead, keep me in love with what's unafraid
to open: daisy heads struck dumb by cold, those few frail buds whose ears are tuned
like mine to some voice alluringly out of season.

Caravan

Dearest one, how could I forget
how long this jaunt has lasted?

We crossed and recrossed the little
passages, shielded the small

golden flowers from the approaching
haboob. We argued with the moon

and her hundred incarnations.
No one drowned on our watch,

only stumbled from craning up
so much toward the darkness.

I think it is no weakness
to confess our love

of starry configurations,
how we plot our movements

by the shambled remnants
of their distant light.

Is the sparrow happier than we are? Is the crow?

Is the sparrow happier than we are? Is the crow?
        The birds tumble and cry through the bushes;
all morning they sing or make that noise we identify
        as *singing*. They come close sometimes:
close enough to touch, to take
        snapshots of, close enough to make us draw
into uncharacteristic stillness for this reward—
        sight of that small pulse beneath a gloss
of feathers, its rapid, tender skitter.
        Scattering riff in the trees as they leave,
and we turn back to tending our own crumb.

Mindful

The wind plays in the accordion
branches. An icy rain pelts the road.
The seed rattles in its pod
the only mantra that it knows.

ACKNOWLEDGMENTS

"Ghazal, with Cow Burial," in *CHA*, December 2017

"Who was your first love?" in *CHA*, December 2017

"Because of global warming," in *The Common*, November 2015

Early versions of the poems in this volume have appeared on *Via Negativa* www.vianegativa.us

---

Gratitude to Elizabeth Adams and Phoenicia Publishing for your faith in these poems; to Dave Bonta, for endless space and support at *Via Negativa*; to Ira Sukrungruang, Aimee Nezhukumatathil, Ivy Alvarez, Satya Robyn, and Tom Montgomery Fate, for your good, strong words; to Marc Neys (Swoon) for the beautiful book trailer; to friends and readers who have cheered these "Buddha" poems onward for the last couple of years; and to my poetry students, who teach me so much every day of my teaching life. *Agyamanac unay.*

ABOUT THE AUTHOR

Luisa A. Igloria is the winner of the 2015 Resurgence Prize (UK), the world's first major award for ecopoetry, selected by former UK poet laureate Sir Andrew Motion, Alice Oswald, and Jo Shapcott. She is the author of the chapbooks *Haori* (Tea & Tattered Pages Press, 2017), *Check & Balance* (Moria Press/Locofo Chaps, 2017), and *Bright as Mirrors Left in the Grass* (Kudzu House Press eChapbook selection for Spring 2015); plus the full length works *Ode to the Heart Smaller than a Pencil Eraser* (selected by Mark Doty for the 2014 May Swenson Prize, Utah State University Press), *Night Willow* (Phoenicia Publishing, Montreal, 2014), *The Saints of Streets* (University of Santo Tomas Publishing House, 2013), *Juan Luna's Revolver* (2009 Ernest Sandeen Prize, University of Notre Dame Press), and nine other books. She teaches on the faculty of the MFA Creative Writing Program at Old Dominion University, which she directed from 2009-2015. Her website is www.luisaigloria.com

CONTRIBUTING AUTHOR

Ira Sukrungruang is a Chicago born Thai-American and the author of the memoirs *Southside Buddhist* and *Talk Thai: The Adventures of Buddhist Boy*; the poetry collection *In Thailand It Is Night*; and the short story collection, *The Melting Season*. He is a professor of English at the University of South Florida, Tampa.

A NOTE ON THE TYPE

The interior text typeface is Adobe Garamond Pro, designed by Robert Slimbach in 1989 as an interpretation of original roman and italic faces by the French type designers Claude Garamond (1505-1561) and Robert Granjon (1530-1590). The display typeface is Helvetica Neue (Light Extended), designed in 1983 by the German typographic foundry D. Stempel AG for Linotype.

ABOUT PHOENICIA PUBLISHING

Phoenicia Publishing is an independent press based in Montreal but involved, through a network of online connections, with writers and artists all over the world. We are interested in words and images that illuminate culture, spirit, and the human experience. A particular focus is on writing and art about travel between cultures—whether literally, through lives of refugees, immigrants, and travelers, or more metaphorically and philosophically—with the goal of enlarging our understanding of one another through universal and particular experiences of change, displacement, disconnection, assimilation, sorrow, gratitude, longing and hope.

We are committed to the innovative use of the web and digital technology in all aspects of publishing and distribution, and to making high-quality works available that might not be viable for larger publishers. We work closely with our authors, and are pleased to be able to offer them a greater share of royalties than is normally possible.

Your support of this endeavor is greatly appreciated.

Our complete catalogue is online at www.phoeniciapublishing.com, where readers can also subscribe to our quarterly newsletter.

CPSIA information can be obtained
at www.ICGtesting.com
Printed in the USA
BVHW03s0733300318
511967BV00010B/20/P